Weather Watch

Lightning

by Jenny Fretland VanVoorst

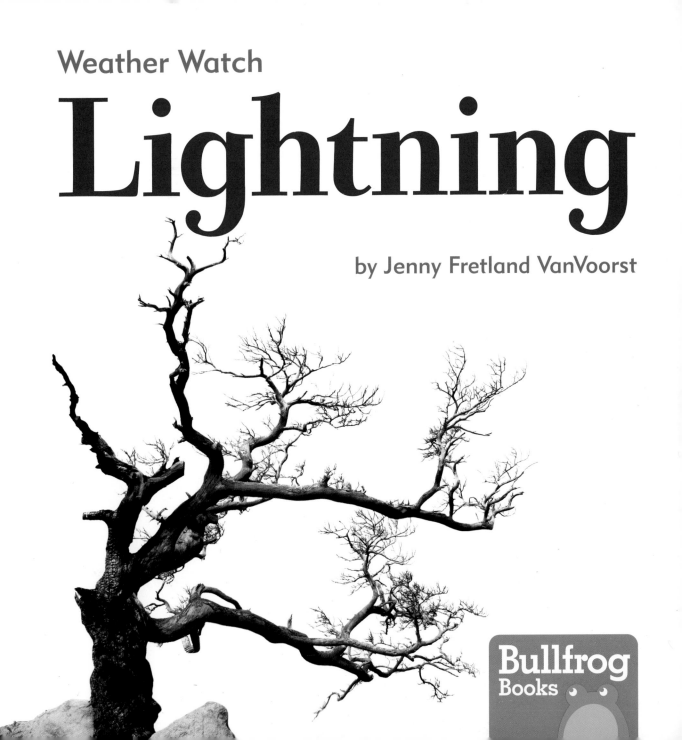

Bullfrog Books

Ideas for Parents and Teachers

Bullfrog Books let children practice reading informational text at the earliest reading levels. Repetition, familiar words, and photo labels support early readers.

Before Reading

- Discuss the cover photo. What does it tell them?

- Look at the picture glossary together. Read and discuss the words.

Read the Book

- "Walk" through the book and look at the photos. Let the child ask questions. Point out the photo labels.

- Read the book to the child, or have him or her read independently.

After Reading

- Prompt the child to think more. Ask: Have you ever seen a lightning storm? How many different kinds of lightning did you see?

Bullfrog Books are published by Jump!
5357 Penn Avenue South
Minneapolis, MN 55419
www.jumplibrary.com

Library of Congress Cataloging-in-Publication Data

Names: Fretland VanVoorst, Jenny, 1972– author.
Title: Lightning / by Jenny Fretland VanVoorst.
Description: Minneapolis, MN: Jump!, Inc. [2016]
© 2017 | Series: Weather watch
Audience: Ages 5–8. | Audience: K to grade 3.
Includes bibliographical references and index.
Identifiers: LCCN 2016014185 (print)
LCCN 2016014583 (ebook)
ISBN 9781620313893 (hardcover: alk. paper)
ISBN 9781624964367 (ebook)
Subjects: LCSH: Lightning—Juvenile literature.
Severe storms—Juvenile literature.
Classification: LCC QC966.5 .F74 2016 (print)
LCC QC966.5 (ebook) | DDC 551.56/32—dc23
LC record available at http://lccn.loc.gov/2016014185

Editor: Kirsten Chang
Series Designer: Ellen Huber
Book Designer: Molly Ballanger
Photo Researcher: Olympia Shannon

Photo Credits: All photos by Shutterstock except:
Alamy, 19, 22br; Dreamstime, 14–15; Getty, 3, 5,
20–21; iStock, 1, 11, 23tr; Thinkstock, 1, 4;
123RF, 10, 23bl.

Printed in the United States of America at
Corporate Graphics in North Mankato, Minnesota.

Table of Contents

Zap! Pow!

Zap!

What is that?

Lightning.

It is a bright
flash in the sky.

You see it when
it storms.

What causes it?

Air swirls
inside a cloud.

What are clouds
made of?

Ice crystals.
Water droplets.

droplet

ice crystals

Moving air rubs
them together.

It makes electricity.

Zap! That's lightning.

Usually it strikes
the ground.

It branches
out like a tree.

It can zap
inside a cloud.

The cloud
lights up.

It can jump to
a new cloud, too.

Pow!

What is that?

Thunder.

What causes it?

Lightning heats the air.
The hot air blows up.
It makes a loud sound.

Zap! Pow!

Lightning is cool.

Types of Lightning

cloud to ground
This kind of lightning goes from the cloud to the ground.

intra-cloud
This kind of lightning flashes inside a cloud.

cloud to cloud
This kind of lightning jumps from one cloud to another.

ball lightning
This rare kind of lightning appears as a large ball of light in the sky.

22

Picture Glossary

crystal
A solid material that has a regularly repeating structure.

electricity
A form of energy found in nature, created by rubbing two unlike things together.

droplets
Very small drops.

strike
To hit.

Index

To Learn More

Learning more is as easy as 1, 2, 3.

1) Go to www.factsurfer.com

2) Enter "lightning" into the search box.

3) Click the "Surf" button to see a list of websites.

With factsurfer.com, finding more information is just a click away.